THE LORD BE WITH YOU

Introducing the Mass to Children

Jenny Pate
DIOCESE OF LANCASTER

Illustrated by Paula Knock

McCrimmons
Great Wakering   Essex

First published in Great Britain in 1997 by
McCrimmon Publishing Co. Ltd.
10-12 High Street Great Wakering Essex SS3 0EQ
Telephone (01702) 218956   Fax (01702) 216082
Email: mccrimmons@dial.pipex.com

ISBN 0 85597 579 2

© 1997 Jenny Pate / Diocese of Lancaster

ACKNOWLEDGEMENTS

Excerpts from the English translation of *The Roman Missal* © 1973, International Committee on English in the Liturgy , Inc. (ICEL); the English translation of Eucharistic Prayer for Masses with Children III from *Eucharistic Prayers for Masses with Children* © 1975, ICEL. All rights reserved.

Authorised by the National Liturgical Commission for England and Wales.

Kevin Mayhew Ltd, Rattlesden, Bury St Edmunds, Suffolk IP30 0SZ, for the words and music of *'Blest be you Lord God of all Creation'* by Aniceto Nazareth. Reproduced by permission.

All the songs used in this publication can be found in *The Complete Celebration Hymnal*, *Celebration Hymnal for Everyone* and *A Year of Celebration*. All published by McCrimmon Publishing Co. Ltd.

Every effort has been made to trace the owners of copyright material and we hope that no copyright has been infringed. Pardon is sought and apology made if the contrary be the case, and a correction will be made in any reprint of this book.

Edited by Eileen Burzynska
Illustrations by Paula Knock
Cover design and text page layout by Nick Snode
Typeset in ITC Symbol Roman 12/14.4(auto)
Printed by BPC Wheatons Ltd, Exeter, Devon
Text printed on Fineblade 90gsm, cover printed on Invercote 240gsm
Repro by Anagram Litho Ltd, Southend-on-Sea, Essex

Contents

Introduction		5
An Overview of this Developmental Approach		8
One	– Introductory Rites with adults	11
Two	– Introducing the "Introductory Rites to Children"	13
Three	– Liturgy of the Word with adults	17
Four	– Introducing the Liturgy of the Word to children	19
Five	– Introducing the Liturgy of the Eucharist to children – preamble	23
Six	– Liturgy of the Eucharist	26
Seven	– Preparation for an act of worship based on the Preparation of the Gifts	29
Eight	– Act of worship based on the Preparation of the Gifts	31
Nine	– Preparation for an act of worship based on the Preface of Eucharistic Prayer 3 with children (outside Easter season)	34
Ten	– Act of worship using the preface	36

Eleven	– Preparation for an act of worship based on the first part of Eucharistic Prayer 3 with children	40
Twelve	– Act of Worship based on the first part of Eucharistic Prayer 3 with children	43
Thirteen	– Preparation for an act of worship based on the final part of Eucharistic Prayer 3 with children	46
Fourteen	– Act of worship based on the final part of the Eucharistic Prayer 3 with children	48
Fifteen	– Eucharistic Prayer with Children III	52
Sixteen	– Communion Rite with adults	57
Seventeen	– Communion Rite with children	61
Eighteen	– Preparing the Communion Rite with children	63
Nineteen	– Act of worship based on the Communion Rite	66
Twenty	– Concluding Rite with adults	71
Twenty One	– Concluding Rite with children (blessings)	73
Music resource section		75

(This includes suggested songs and settings in A Year of Celebration and Celebration Hymnal for Everyone for use in the liturgies)

Introduction

For eighteen years as a primary teacher and about as many years as a parish catechist I have arranged countless Masses for children on their own and for children with adults.

Many people regarded these occasions as successful. I was not so sure then and I am even less convinced now. Lively singing, colourful pictures and moving dramas (often disastrously staged) did much to eliminate boredom but offered little by way of real prayer and real celebration. The principal ingredient was absent, by and large we were the unconverted. We had nothing to celebrate. We had no song in our hearts, so we had no song to sing.

It is chiefly for this reason that I have not responded to many teachers' and catechists' requests for materials setting out Mass themes suitable for children and the adults in their lives. To do so would be to start at the end rather than the beginning. Whilst lively liturgies do much to encourage attendance, alone they do not solve the problem of diminishing attention and declining Mass attendance. Regular attendance at the celebration of the Eucharist is a sign of mature commitment, not necessarily the means towards such commitment.

Some schools, especially primary schools, feel they should remedy the problem by regularly taking children to church for Mass (often each week); a view sometimes shared by parishioners and some clergy who are

THE LORD BE WITH YOU

reassured by such sights, confident that if children come often enough, "they will get used to coming" and "if the children come, so will their parents". This approach does not help and sometimes causes damage.

Mass is primarily an adult celebration which despite adaptations leaves most children bewildered. They may join in the songs, some prayers, stand and sit at all the appropriate times and appear to participate but they remain very much on the edge. This level of involvement may seem acceptable to some children during their early primary years but, by the time they reach the later primary years, their patience is at an end. They stop attending Mass. There are, of course, always exceptions. But it remains the case that, when asked, most Catholic schools report that less than 10% of their pupils regularly attend Mass.

What can schools do?

The work of evangelisation needs prominence. Baptism does not bring about instant conversion. Conversion is a slow business, which will not be achieved by manipulated attendance at Mass.

Schools are among the most well placed agencies in the church for this work. They are able to establish often long-lasting relationships with the families they serve. They are able to witness to the Christian life through the lifestyle and teaching of their staff, governors and some parents.

Schools can contribute particularly to this slow process of conversion, through regular acts of worship based on the Liturgy of the Word. It is through the Word of God that we come to a deeper more personal awareness of God's plan of salvation through Jesus Christ. The Liturgy of the Word is fundamental to prayer and worship, particularly so in school. Schools are places concerned with words. The Word of God has a central place in a Catholic school.

Introduction

How can we bring children to an understanding of the Mass?

The following pages explain and illustrate a way of introducing young children to the celebration of the Eucharist. The step by step approach adopted fits in with current educational practice. Just as schools begin with simple number work and familiarisation with story books, before moving on to higher level tasks in mathematics and reading, so too children can be introduced to parts of the celebration of the Eucharist, first simply, then in a more developed way in later years.

It is my hope that by giving children a manageable amount, in a style appropriate to their stage of development, their capacity for understanding the Celebration of the Eucharist may grow.

This book aims to bring children and their teachers to a deeper understanding of the Celebration of the Eucharist. It offers activities and liturgies suitable for schools' daily acts of worship, based on the Mass.

It is dedicated to all teachers and parish catechists, who like myself, are tired and frustrated with exercising the "ministry of the glare" to children during Mass. It is also dedicated to all children who have been recipients of this ministry. Sorry!

An Overview of this Developmental Approach

With this approach

**Children aged 5–7 years old
will, through experience,**

> become familiar with the INTRODUCTORY RITES
> become familiar with the LITURGY OF THE WORD (acclamation and gospel)
> become familiar with the CONCLUDING RITES
>
> and at 7 years of age some parts of the EUCHARISTIC PRAYER, some parts of the COMMUNION RITE.

**Children aged 7–9 years old
will, through experience,**

> become familiar with all elements of the INTRODUCTORY RITES
> become familiar with all essential elements of the LITURGY OF THE WORD
> become familiar with the EUCHARISTIC PRAYER (for children)
> become familiar with the COMMUNION RITE
> become familiar with the CONCLUDING RITE

An Overview of this Developmental Approach

Children aged 10+11 years old will, through experience,

>become familiar with all elements of the INTRODUCTORY RITES
>become familiar with all elements of the LITURGY OF THE WORD
>>(including some non-adapted texts)
>
>become familiar with the EUCHARISTIC PRAYER (for children)
>become familiar with the COMMUNION RITE
>become familiar with the CONCLUDING RITE
>
>and have experience of the full eucharistic celebration.

Whole School Celebrations

Introducing children to the eucharist in this way does not exclude the celebration of the eucharist with the whole school.

If the whole school gathers together to celebrate Mass from time to time, consider allowing:

>5+6 year olds to lead the INTRODUCTORY RITE and the CONCLUDING RITE
>
>10+11 year olds to lead the LITURGY OF THE WORD
>
>7+8 year olds to contribute visuals, actions and music during the EUCHARISTIC PRAYER
>
>9 year olds to take some leadership during the COMMUNION RITE.

Teachers, parents, governors and clergy should, however, consider the frequency of such full eucharist liturgical celebrations, given the age, aptitude and faith backgrounds of the pupils in their care.

One

Introductory Rites with Adults

The purpose of these rites is to make those present into one community and to prepare them to listen to God's word and to celebrate the Eucharist.

The INTRODUCTORY RITES include:

ENTRANCE ANTIPHON
(See Music resource section on Page 75 for suggestions)

This should be sung rather than spoken. It is often replaced by a hymn. This entrance song should only last as long as it takes the celebrant to reach the sanctuary. A repeated chorus might fit the bill more easily than a lengthy hymn. Whatever is used should not take up an excessive amount of time; the time and effort for this first action should not be disproportionate to the rest of the celebration.

WELCOME

The welcome and grace is said by the celebrant and may take the simple form of the Sign of the Cross.
Some words introducing the theme of the celebration may follow.
These can be said by the celebrant or a lay person.

The Lord be with you

Penitential Rite   *(This can be sung – see Music resource section)*
We make our peace with God and each other. The emphasis is on the mercy of God and on our dependence on God rather than on our own personal sin.
This rite concludes with words of absolution said by the celebrant.

Gloria   *(This should be sung – see Music resource section)*
This is a hymn of joy and praise. It is not obligatory, though it should not always be left out (except during Advent and Lent).

Opening Prayer / First Prayer / Collect
A short prayer drawing together the intentions of all present. This is said by the celebrant. It may be written by the celebrant or those preparing the liturgy. It relates to the theme of the celebration.

Two

Introducing the "Introductory Rites to Children"

As the intention of these rites is to prepare those gathered to celebrate God's word, it can reasonably be argued that they should not be separated from the Liturgy of the Word. This is true. Yet anyone with experience of working with young children will recognise some similarities between these rites and the gathering rituals of the school day.

With occasional acts of collective worship, based on a similar pattern, relating to the tasks of the day, we can begin to give children some insight into the meaning and purpose of these rites as well as some experience of celebrating them.

5 + 6 Year Olds

A GATHERING SONG (*see Music resource section*) and an OPENING PRAYER, in an informal setting, such as on the mat, or in a more formal setting such as the school hall, is already common practice in many schools.

An exemplar prayer for this age group:

Let us pray,
> God our Father, watch over us in school today
> keep us safe, help us to be happy
> and behave just like your Son, Jesus,
> *(as confidence and understanding grows add)...*
> We ask this through our Lord Jesus Christ. Amen.

THE LORD BE WITH YOU

When some simple understanding of the Trinity has been achieved add:

> We ask this through our Lord Jesus Christ, your Son, who lives and reigns with you and the Holy Spirit, one God, for ever and ever. Amen.

7 Year Olds+

Other elements may be introduced. The act of worship might now include a PENITENTIAL RITE and the GLORIA [or similar song/prayer].
(*See Music resource section*)

An exemplar penitential rite for this age group:

> Blessed are you, Lord Jesus,
>   your love is everlasting.
> Lord have mercy.
> R. Lord have mercy.
>
> Blessed are you, Lord Jesus,
>   you came to forgive our sins.
> Christ have mercy.
> R. Christ have mercy.
>
> Blessed are you, Lord Jesus,
>   you teach us how to forgive.
> Lord have mercy.
> R. Lord have mercy.

All
> May God be good to us, forgive us all we have done wrong and make us happy with him in our home in heaven.

Child or adult
> Let us now give thanks and praise to God our Father for his gift of forgiveness.

GLORIA... *(prayer or song)*

Two – Introducing the "Introductory Rites to Children"

10 Year Old+

The children should now be familiar with the elements and pattern of the Introductory Rites of the Mass. At this age the rites should only be celebrated in context, i.e. with the Liturgy of the Word.

N.B. "If there is no song in the heart, there is no song to be sung."

The success of such acts of worship depend on the children's experience of forgiveness in school and their having real reasons for songs of joy and praise.

Three

Liturgy of the Word with Adults

FIRST READING
(read by a lay person)

> The reading focuses on the story of God's relationship with his people. It is usually from the Old Testament.

PSALM
(this should be sung – see Music resource section)

> The psalm is our reply… Yes! It's our experience too!

SECOND READING
(read by a lay person)

> It focuses on the story of the early church, often from a letter circulated in the early church, sometimes accounts of the apostles' activities. It does not always have an apparently clear connection with the Gospel.
> It may be omitted at any time.

ACCLAMATION
(must be sung and best accompanied with a short procession of the Book of the Gospels to the lectern.)

> We welcome the words of Jesus.

GOSPEL
(read by a deacon or a priest)

   Jesus' Story; Our Story

HOMILY
(usually given by a priest)

   What is this saying to our experience? Where do we go from here?

CREED
(Said by all, sometimes replaced by renewal of baptismal vows or a baptism.)

   We believe, we commit ourselves to God.

INTERCESSIONS
(read by a lay person)

   Call to prayer. We ask God to help us to live out his story today. These prayers (about four) are a direct response to the Gospel.

Four

Introducing the "Liturgy of the Word" to children

This part of the Mass can be greatly adapted when celebrated with children. The Gospel is the only obligatory reading.

Once again, there are clear step-by-step ways of gradually introducing children to the full celebration of this rite.

The Liturgy of the Word can easily stand on its own as a distinct celebration.

5 + 6 Year Olds

A celebration of the Word might consist of:

A simplified sung ACCLAMATION, one that might be used in the children's Liturgy of the Word celebration during Sunday Mass:

THE LORD BE WITH YOU

second voice starts at B when sung as a round.

A simplified GOSPEL

A short HOMILY. Perhaps some intercessions.

7 Year Olds +

A celebration of the Word might consist of:

A short simplified FIRST READING

PSALM
(A song of thanksgiving/hope/joy/commitment/anguish/promise/may be appropriate. It should be a heartfelt response to the first reading.)

ACCLAMATION

A SIMPLIFIED GOSPEL

A short HOMILY and some INTERCESSIONS

10 Year Olds +

By now many, or most, of the children have reached a level in their English studies, by which they have some understanding of different literary styles. Such children are ready to celebrate fully the Liturgy of the Word, possibly using some adult texts, particularly for the Gospel.

CREED

> The creed is not usually said at week day Masses. For those schools wishing to introduce the creed in a simple form the following examples are given.
>
> I believe in you, O God
> I believe in God the Father who is making all things.
> I believe in Jesus the Son
> I believe in the Spirit of Jesus who helps us to love.
> Amen.
>
> ---
>
> O God,
> I believe that you made the whole world.
> I believe that Jesus is God and man,
> and died on the cross for me.
>
> I believe the Spirit of Jesus lives on
> and remains with us.

I believe the Spirit of Jesus lives on
and remains with us.

I believe in one holy Church.

I believe through Jesus sins are forgiven.

I believe the Spirit of Jesus will help me
to build heaven on earth.

I believe that one day I will be happy in heaven. Amen.

A simplified creed might contain separate verses on the following subjects: Trinity, Creation, Incarnation, Redemption, Church and the Coming of the Kingdom.

Since the creed is such a confessional prayer, it may be inappropriate for some children.

N.B. Success with the Liturgy of the Word depends on the children's experience and use of scripture. Schools thoroughly covering the "Here I Am" programme or similar will be well placed for such celebrations.

I have not offered any examples of liturgies of the word with simplified texts. There are many simplified scripture texts available, some already arranged in themes.

Five

Introducing the Liturgy of the Eucharist to children – Preamble

A great deal of thought and preparation goes into planning and preparing the Introductory Rites and the Liturgy of the Word. These parts of the Mass give the greatest scope for lay involvement.

Once these parts are concluded, with the exception of musicians, those responsible for preparation of the liturgy now breath a sigh of relief. With the safe arrival of the offertory gifts and the last chorus of the offertory hymn, teachers now adjourn to exercise the ministry of the glare!

It is not just teachers, parents too exercise this ministry, in between acts of bribery which they hope will persuade their children to be still and quiet just a while longer. Priests make desperate attempts

THE LORD BE WITH YOU

to engage children's attention by raising their voices, making exaggerated gestures or, by simply rushing on, relying on teachers and parents to maintain order.

A solution often offered is an invitation to gather around the altar until the Sign of Peace. This certainly quietens many and, sometimes, it appears as if the children's attention is actually engaged, though I wonder. The eucharistic prayers have lost the attention of many an adult.

A child I once knew referred to these prayers as the "everlasting prayer". Her sighs made clear that she was not referring to it as part of eucharistic celebrations generation after generation.

Eucharist Prayers for Masses where children are in the majority

Since 1973 three eucharistic prayers for Masses celebrated with children were issued by the Sacred Congregation for Divine Worship. Sadly, they are rarely used. Some priests tell me that they dislike them, whether it is because they personally find them unsatisfying, or whether they find children dislike them, I am not too sure.

Whatever the shortcomings of these prayers, they make much more sense to children (and some adults) than the four eucharistic prayers currently used. Reciting the words of these prayers alone does not make them meaningful. Just as poetry needs time, contemplation, discussion and familiarisation, so do these prayers.

Eucharistic Prayer for Children 3 (outside the Easter Season)

I have taken what appears to children as an "elephant-sized" prayer and have broken it down into "bite-sized" pieces, enough for a school act of worship. I have included some "before activities" too.

Five – Introducing the Liturgy of the Eucharist to children – Preamble

My reasons for choosing this prayer are that, although it is a little longer than the others, and the language a little more difficult, it is the one used most frequently and has language which is also used in the standard eucharistic prayers.

Six

Liturgy of the Eucharist

Begins with PREPARATION OF THE ALTAR AND THE GIFTS with Adults.

OFFERTORY SONG AND PROCESSION

A suitable song that the whole congregation can sing whilst the gifts are brought to the altar. Gifts of charity (children's work) should be presented first, then the bread and wine.

PREPARATION OF THE GIFTS

The priest, standing at the altar, takes the paten with the bread and, holding it slightly raised above the altar, says quietly:

> Blessed are you, Lord of all creation.
> Through your goodness we have this bread to offer,
> which earth has given and human hands have made.
> It will become for us the bread of life.

Then he places the paten with the bread on the corporal (a white square cloth).

> R. **Blessed be God for ever.**

The deacon (or priest) pours wine and a little water into the chalice saying quietly.

Six – Liturgy of the Eucharist

By the mystery of this water and wine, may we come to share
in the divinity of Christ, who humbled himself
to share our humanity.

Then taking the chalice and holding it slightly raised above the altar, he says quietly:

Blessed are, Lord, God of all creation.
Through your goodness we have this wine to offer,
fruit of the vine and work of human hands.
It will become our spiritual drink.

Then he places the chalice on the corporal.

R. **Blessed be God for ever.**

The priest bows and says quietly:

Lord God, we ask you to receive us and be pleased
with the sacrifice we offer you
with humble and contrite hearts.

Standing at the side of the altar he washes his hands saying:

Lord wash away my iniquity; cleanse me from my sin.

Standing at the centre of the altar, facing the people, he extends and then joins his hands, saying:

Pray, brethren, that our sacrifice may be acceptable
to God, the almighty Father.

R. **May the Lord accept the sacrifice at your hands
for the praise and glory of his name,
for our good and the good of all his Church.**

THE LORD BE WITH YOU

PRAYER OVER THE GIFTS
This short prayer relates to the theme.

An exemplar:

> Lord God
> we offer you these gifts of bread and wine
> and with them our whole life.
> May they make us holy
> so that one day we will be with you
> in your kingdom.
> We ask this through Christ our Lord.

With Children

The same pattern follows.

OFFERTORY SONG AND PROCESSION

PREPARATION OF THE GIFTS
Sometimes this is substituted with a song   *(See Music resource section)*

PRAYER OVER THE GIFTS
(When studying this part of the Mass, familiarise the children with the priest's actions.)

NOTICE
Bread for nourishment, wine for joy.
Water and wine mixed, representing Jesus' humanity and divinity which we hope to share.

The washing of hands
The raising of the paten and chalice to help focus our attention.

Seven

Preparation for an Act of Worship based on the Preparation of the Gifts

a few days in advance of the act of worship

With younger children from about 6 years +

Ask them to collect three sets of items:

> Items that God alone created, such as a rock;
> Items that they helped God create, such as planted cress seeds;
> Items that they had quite a bit to do with creating, such as a piece of written work.

Watch the collections grow either in the classroom or hall.

With older children from about 9 years +

Give each a blank piece of paper. Ask this question,

> "How clever are people? What can they make? What can't they make?"

THE LORD BE WITH YOU

Give them some time, as long as they need to think, before committing their ideas to paper in words, symbols or pictures. Some will seek reassurance, "How many lines do we write? Do we write about... ? Do we put the date? etc." Do not give any clues. Emphasis that the answer is whatever they think.

Eight
Act of Worship

Display your collections:

> GOD ALONE CREATED
> CREATION WE HELPED GOD WITH A BIT
> THINGS WE CREATED WITH GOD'S HELP

Child A lists the items in the first collection.
Child B lists the items in the second collection.
Child C lists the items in the third collection.

A small number of children share their responses to the question, "How clever are people?"

Choose an appropriate song to accompany the following: (*See Music resource section*)

Two children now process through the hall/classroom carrying a plate of bread and a glass of wine. They stand facing the children in front of the collections until the song has finished.

PREPARATION OF THE GIFTS

The teacher asks: Which collection do these belong to?

When the children have answered, place them in the appropriate spot.

THE LORD BE WITH YOU

Sing: Blessed be God

Eight – Act of Worship

2 Blest are you, Lord, God of all creation,
thanks to your goodness this wine we offer:
fruit of the earth, work of our hands,
it will become the cup of life.

*"Blessed be God" by Aniceto Nazareth © Kevin Mayhew Ltd.
Reproduced by permission from Hymns Old and New*

Conclude with a **PRAYER OVER THE GIFTS**

Everyone:

> Lord God,
> We offer you these gifts of bread and wine
> and with them our whole life.
> May we use our talents and creation wisely
> so that together with you
> we build your kingdom here on earth.
> We ask this through your Son
> Jesus Christ our Lord.

It may be necessary to explain beforehand to some children what is meant by "The Kingdom of God on earth". Explain that it is the world and all the people living in it, in the manner God intended.

Nine

Eucharistic Prayer 3 with Children
(This prayer can be found written out in full on p.52)

These short liturgies, based on the EUCHARISTIC PRAYER 3 WITH CHILDREN, are to enable children to reflect on, pray and become familiar with this prayer, outside the celebration of the eucharist. The activities, actions and spoken parts here cannot be a substitute for any part of this prayer during a celebration of Mass.

Preparation for an act of worship based on the preface to Eucharistic Prayer 3 with children (outside the Easter season)

A DAY OR TWO IN ADVANCE

(a) With children 6–11 years old

Give each child a blank piece of paper, ask them to write or draw, "What makes you happy?" (Again, with reassurance that the only right answer is their answer.)

Nine – Eucharistic Prayer 3 with Children

Give each child another piece of paper, this time asking "What makes you sad?"

Share your thoughts with each other. Choose some children willing to share their thoughts more publicly.

Later, learn by heart:

The responses in the first part of the act of worship and the prayer beginning "Holy, holy, holy Lord…"

Bring to the children's attention that the first line and response to this act of worship signals the beginning of a special part when spoken in the Mass.

(b) With children 9–11 years old

An extension activity to deepen their appreciation of the words of Child: A – (see p.37)

Give each child a slip of paper, divide them into four groups, ask one group to write DEAF on their slip of paper, another to write BLIND on their paper, another DUMB and the other group CAN'T MOVE.

Put all the slips of paper into a bag/box and invite each child to take a slip of paper with their eyes closed.

When the act of worship begins, that is how they must behave.

Ten

Act of Worship

Using the words of the preface of the Eucharistic Prayer for Children 3

*If using activity (b) from previous page, before you begin, give the children blindfolds, ear plugs, etc., according to whatever disability came out of the bag.

> Group A. The Lord be with you.
> Group B. **And also with you.**
>
> Group A. Lift up your hearts.
> Group B. **We lift them up to the Lord.**
>
> Group A. Let us give thanks to the Lord our God.
> Group B. **It is right to give him thanks and praise.**

Children share, what makes them happy and what makes them sad. (5 minutes only)

Ten – Act of Worship

Child A+B   We thank you,
            God our Father

Child A   You made us to live for you and for each other.
            We can see and speak to one another,
            and become friends,
            and share our joys and sorrow.

Child B   And so, Father, we gladly thank you
            with everyone who believed in you;
            with the saints and the angels,
            we rejoice and praise you, saying:

(Children may like to raise their arms and hands in praise during this prayer, except those who cannot move. It is meant to be a song of praise and should be sung.)

Everyone:

> Holy, holy, holy Lord, God of power and might,
> heaven and earth are full of your glory.
> Hosanna in the highest.
> Blessed is he who comes in the name of the Lord.
> Hosanna in the highest.

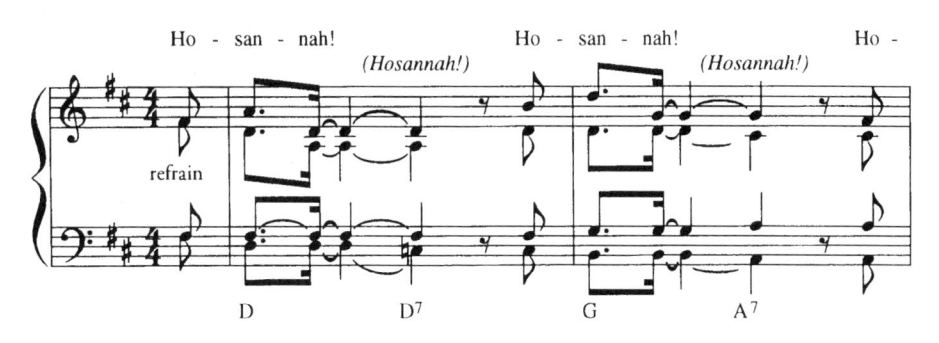

THE LORD BE WITH YOU

Ten – Act of Worship

Holy, Holy: Garfield Rochard © McCrimmon Publishing Co.Ltd.

(For alternative settings, please see *Music resource section*)

Pause, ask child A to repeat his/her verse. Ask the children if they were able to see each other, speak to each other?

Ask them (perhaps returning to class) to think of ways in which this act of worship could be changed to include everyone present. Choose some realistic ideas, implement them and repeat the session.

Eleven

Preparation for an act of worship, based on the first part of the Eucharistic Prayer for Children 3

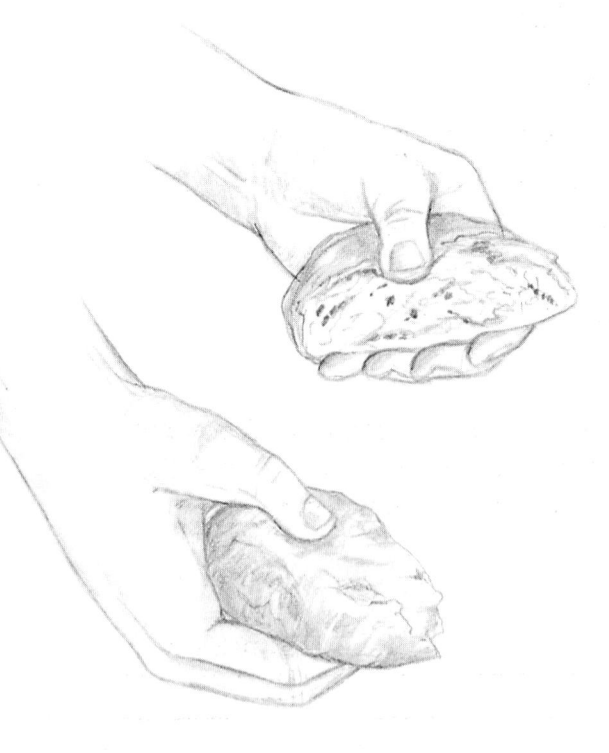

A DAY IN ADVANCE

With children 7–11 years

Remove the children from as many distractions as possible. Ask them to sit perfectly still and to close their eyes.

Once they have settled, ask them to think of someone they would love to have sitting next to them at this moment. It can be anyone they choose, it might be someone they know who doesn't know them; it could be someone who lives on the other side of the world; it could be someone who has died. Pretend they are sitting next to you and talk to them, enjoy their company... for about 5 minutes.

Eleven – Preparation for an act of worship

When the time is up, let the children slowly open their eyes. If any of them appear tearful, perhaps because of painful memories, reassure them that it is O.K. to be sad.

Point out that, through our hearts and minds, we can make people present.

This is one of the ways in which Jesus is present in the eucharist. When we remember him, we remember his words and actions at this last supper. We remember especially what he did with bread and wine. When we do the same, Jesus is present.

With children 6–9 years old

Draw four pictures of Jesus at the Last Supper.

Under the 1st write:	He took bread
Under the 2nd write:	and gave you thanks.
Under the 3rd write:	He broke the bread
Under the 4th write:	and gave it to his friends.

With children 9–11 years old

Explore the words "everlasting covenant".

For "covenant" use "promise" and ask: "What is a promise?" Check out their understanding. Children often confuse promises with secrets. If they understand the difference, let them fill the chart below, first by themselves, then once more as a group.

What is a promise?

	Yes	No	Don't know
Should adults make promises?			
Should children make promises?			
Should promises last forever?			
Is it OK to break a promise?			

THE LORD BE WITH YOU

After they have shared their views, give out copies of the short liturgy that follows. Ask them to find the words "everlasting covenant".
When they have, ask: What was Jesus promising? Will he always keep this promise? (Assure them he will and without any conditions!)

Twelve

Act of Worship based on the first part of the Eucharistic Prayer for Children 3

Gather the children into a circle. Remind them of the two previous short liturgies, place the bread and wine in the centre and remind them that (having attended the previous liturgy) we are now more conscious of each other.

Repeat the memory activity.

We are now going to remember Jesus and something that he did. We are also going to hear how at Mass Jesus becomes present.

Child A   Yes, Lord, you are holy; you are kind to us and to all.
For this we thank you.
We thank you above all for your Son, Jesus Christ.

THE LORD BE WITH YOU

Child B You sent him into this world
because people had turned away from you
and no longer loved each other.
He opened our eyes and our hearts
to understand that we are brothers and sisters
and that you are Father of us all.

Child C He now brings us together to one table
and asks us to do what he did.

At Mass the priest joins his hands and, holding them outstretched over the offerings, says:

Adult Father,
we ask you to bless these gifts of bread and wine
and make them holy.

He then joins his hands and, making the Sign of the Cross once over the chalice, says:

  Change them for us into the body + and blood of
  Jesus Christ, your Son.

With his hands joined, he continues to tell what happened the night before Jesus died. Let us all join our hands as we remember what Jesus did.

Child D On the night before he died for us,
he had supper for the last time with his disciples.

(Whilst children display their pictures)

Child E He took bread
and gave thanks.
He broke the bread
and gave it to his friends, saying:

Child F Take this, all of you, and eat it:
this is my body which will be given up for you.

Child G   In the same way he took a cup of wine.
He gave you thanks
and handed the cup to his disciples, saying:

Child H   Take this, all of you, and drink from it:
this is the cup of my blood,
the blood of the new and everlasting covenant.
It will be shed for you and for all
so that sins may be forgiven.

Everyone **Do this in memory of me.**

Return to quiet moments. This time suggest to the children, as they close their eyes, that it is Jesus they imagine is next to them. They can tell him what is on their mind.

You may wish to finish this short liturgy with some music or a brief, softly-sung song. Whilst parts of the eucharist are sung, it would be inappropriate to sing hymns at any time during this prayer in a full eucharistic celebration.

Thirteen

Preparation for an Act of Worship based on the final part of the Eucharistic Prayer for Children 3

A DAY IN ADVANCE

With children aged 6–11 years old

Make lists:

- a list of all the people who will be attending your act of worship
- a different list, naming all the people you know who do good in the world
- a list naming as many saints as you can.

Find out the name of the pope and the bishop of your diocese.

Those not involved in the above activity can create "Happy Ever After" pictures.

Thirteen – Preparation for an act of worship

With children aged 9–11 years old

In addition to the above, explore the word "sacrifice."

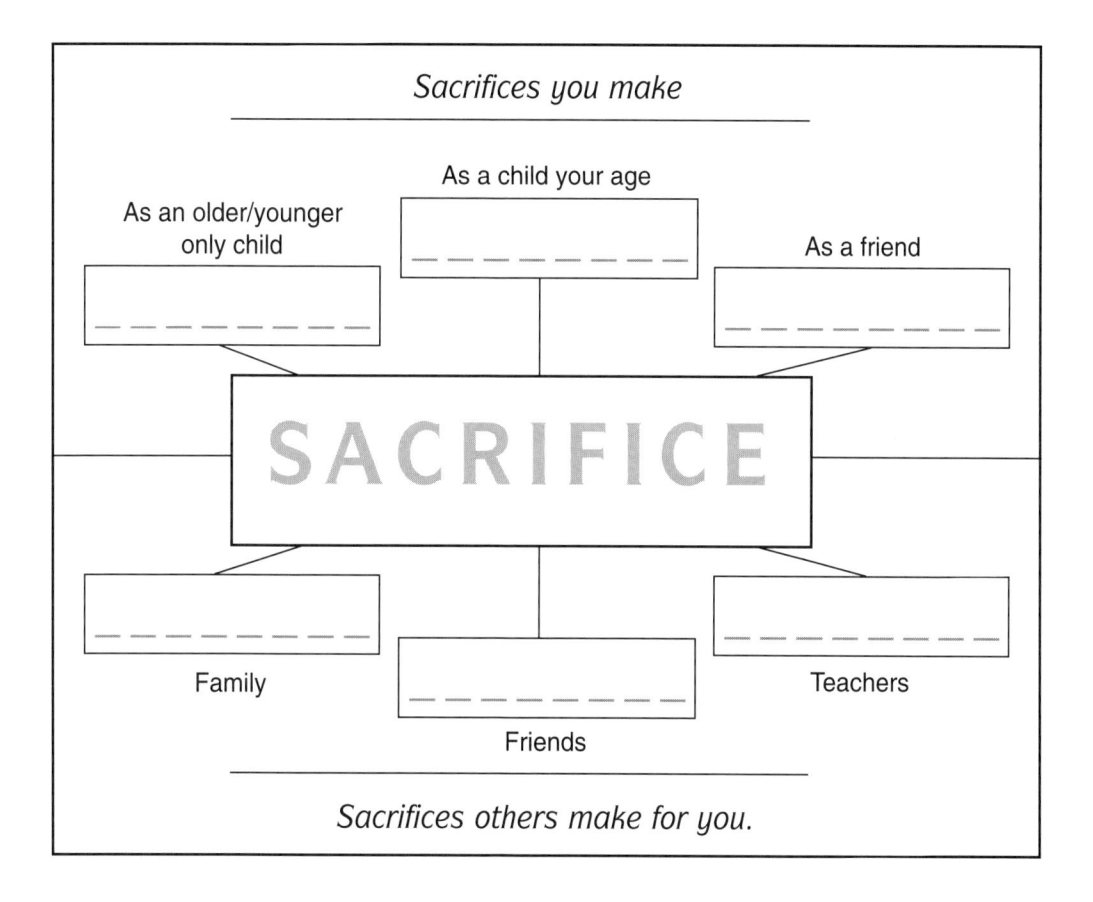

```
Sacrifices you make

As an older/younger          As a child your age
   only child                                              As a friend


                        SACRIFICE


   Family                                                   Teachers
                             Friends
Sacrifices others make for you.
```

Choose other categories if you wish.

Fourteen

Act of Worship based on the final part of the Eucharistic Prayer for Children 3

Invite the older children to say a little about sacrifice

> Child A   God our Father,
> we remember with joy
> all that Jesus did to save us.
> In this holy sacrifice,
> which he gave as a gift to his Church,
> we remember his death and resurrection.

Fourteen – Act of worship

Child B   Father in heaven,
   accept us together with your beloved Son.
   He willingly died for us,
   but you raise him to life again.
   We thank you and say:

Everyone Glory to God in the highest
   (should be sung or replaced with a known sung acclamation)

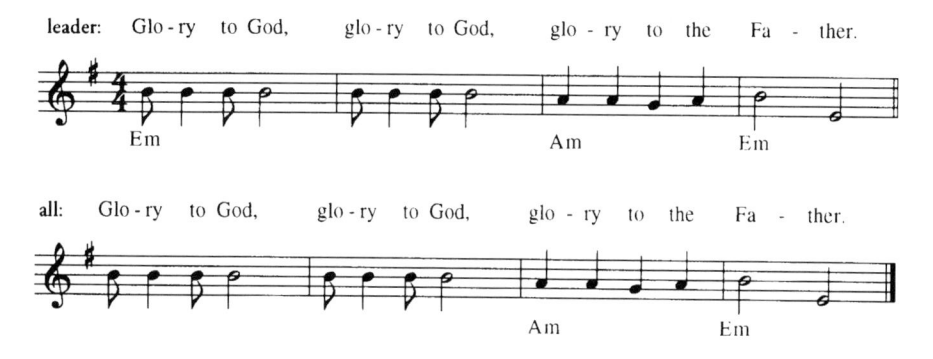

leader: Glo-ry to God, glo-ry to God, glo-ry to the Fa-ther.

all: Glo-ry to God, glo-ry to God, glo-ry to the Fa-ther.

Glory to God: Trad. Peruvian

Child C   Jesus now lives with you in glory,
   but he is also here on earth, among us.
   We thank you and say:

Everyone Glory to God in the highest

leader: Glo-ry to God, glo-ry to God, Son of the Fa-ther.

all: Glo-ry to God, glo-ry to God, Son the the Fa-ther.

Glory to God: Trad. Peruvian

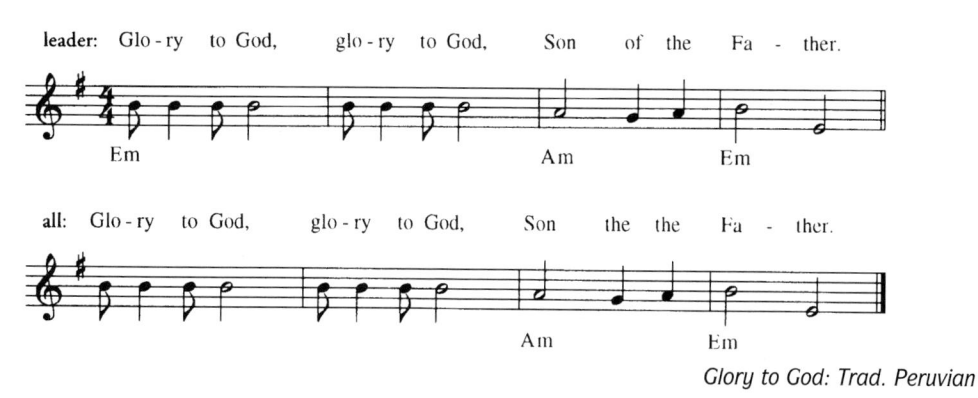

* *Alert children with "Happy Ever After" pictures to be ready to stand.*

THE LORD BE WITH YOU

Child D   One day he will come in glory
and in his kingdom
there will be no more suffering,
no more tears, no more sadness.
We thank you and say:

Everyone Glory to God in the highest

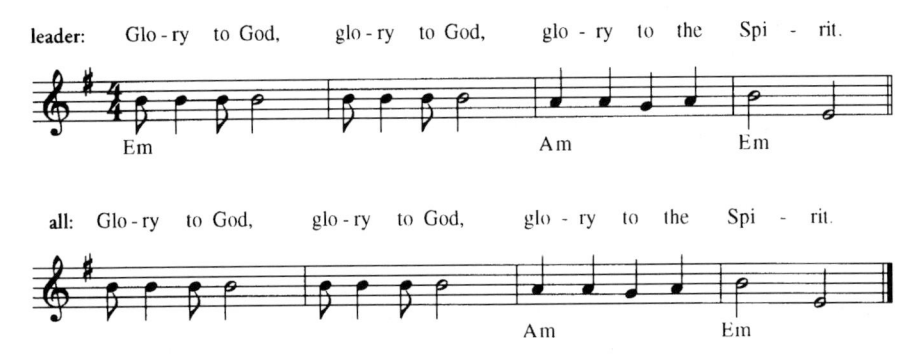

leader: Glo-ry to God, glo-ry to God, glo-ry to the Spi-rit.

Em   Am   Em

all: Glo-ry to God, glo-ry to God, glo-ry to the Spi-rit.

Am   Em

Glory to God: Trad Peruvian

* Alert children with lists to be ready to stand.

Lists of those who are attending this liturgy

Child E   Father in heaven
you have called us
to receive the body and blood of Christ at this table
and to be filled with the joy of the Holy Spirit.
Through this sacred meal
give us strength to please you more and more.

Child F   Lord, our God,
remember n......, our pope and
n......, our bishop.

List of all who do good

Child G   Help all who follow Jesus
to work for peace
and to bring happiness to others.

Fourteen – Act of worship

Lists of all the saints

Child H   Bring us at last
together with Mary, the Mother of God,
and all the saints,
to live with you
and to be one with Christ in heaven.

Group   Through him
with him,
in him,
in the unity of the Holy Spirit
all glory and honour is yours,
almighty Father,
for ever and ever.

Everyone Amen!
(This is an "amen" to the whole prayer: say it as loudly as you can – it should be sung).

leader: Al - le - lu - ia, a - men.   all: Al - le - lu - ia, a - men,

al - le - lu - ia, a - men,   al - le - lu - ia, a - men.

To him be glory for ever: Trad. Peruvian

Fifteen

Eucharistic Prayer with Children 3
(outside the Easter Season)

The Lord be with you.
And also with you

Lift up your hearts.
We lift them up to the Lord.

Let us give thanks to the Lord our God.
It is right to give him thanks and praise.

We thank you,
God our Father.

You made us to live for you and for each other.
We can see and speak to one another,
and become friends,
and share our joys and sorrows.

And so, Father, we gladly thank you
with everyone who believes in you;
with the saints and the angels,
we rejoice and praise you, saying:

**Holy, holy, holy, God of power and might,
heaven and earth are full of your glory.
Hosanna in the highest.**

Blessed is he who comes in the name of the Lord.

Fifteen – Eucharistic Prayer with Children 3

Hosanna in the highest.

Yes, Lord, you are holy;
you are kind to us and to all people.
For this we thank you.
We thank you above all for your Son, Jesus Christ.

You sent him into this world
because people had turned away from you
and no longer loved each other.
He opened our eyes and our hearts
to understand that we are brothers and sisters
and that you are Father of us all.

He now brings us together to one table
and asks us to do what he did.

Father,
we ask you to bless these gifts of bread and wine
and make them holy.

Change them for us into the body + and blood of Jesus Christ, your Son.

On the night before he died for us,
he had supper for the last time with his disciples.

He took bread
and gave you thanks.

He broke the bread and gave it to his friends, saying:

Take this, all of you, and eat it:
this is my body which will be given up for you.

In the same way he took a cup of wine.
He gave you thanks
and handed the cup to his disciples, saying:

Take this, all of you, and drink from it:

this is the cup of my blood,
the blood of the new and everlasting covenant.
It will be shed for you and for all
so that sins may be forgiven.
Do this in memory of me.

God our Father,
we remember with joy
all that Jesus did to save us.
In this holy sacrifice,
which he gave as a gift to his Church,
we remember his death and resurrection.

Father in heaven,
accept us together with your beloved Son.
He willingly died for us,
but you raised him to life again.
We thank you and say:

Glory to God in the highest
(or some other suitable acclamation of praise)

Jesus now lives with you in glory,
but he is also here on earth, among us.
We thank you and say:

Glory to God in the highest.

One day he will come in glory
and in his kingdom
there will be no more suffering,
no more tears, no more sadness.
We thank you and say:

Glory to God in the highest.

Father in heaven,
you have called us
to receive the body and blood of Christ at this table

Fifteen – Eucharistic Prayer with Children 3

and to be filled with the joy of the Holy Spirit.
Through this sacred meal
give us strength to please you more and more.

Lord, our God, remember N...... , our pope,
N...... , our bishop, and all other bishops.

Help all who follow Jesus
to work for peace
and to bring happiness to others.

Bring us all at last
together with Mary, the Mother of God,
and all the saints,
to live with you
and to be one with Christ in heaven.

Through him,
with him,
in him,
in the unity of the Holy Spirit
all glory and honour is yours
almighty Father,
for ever and ever.
Amen

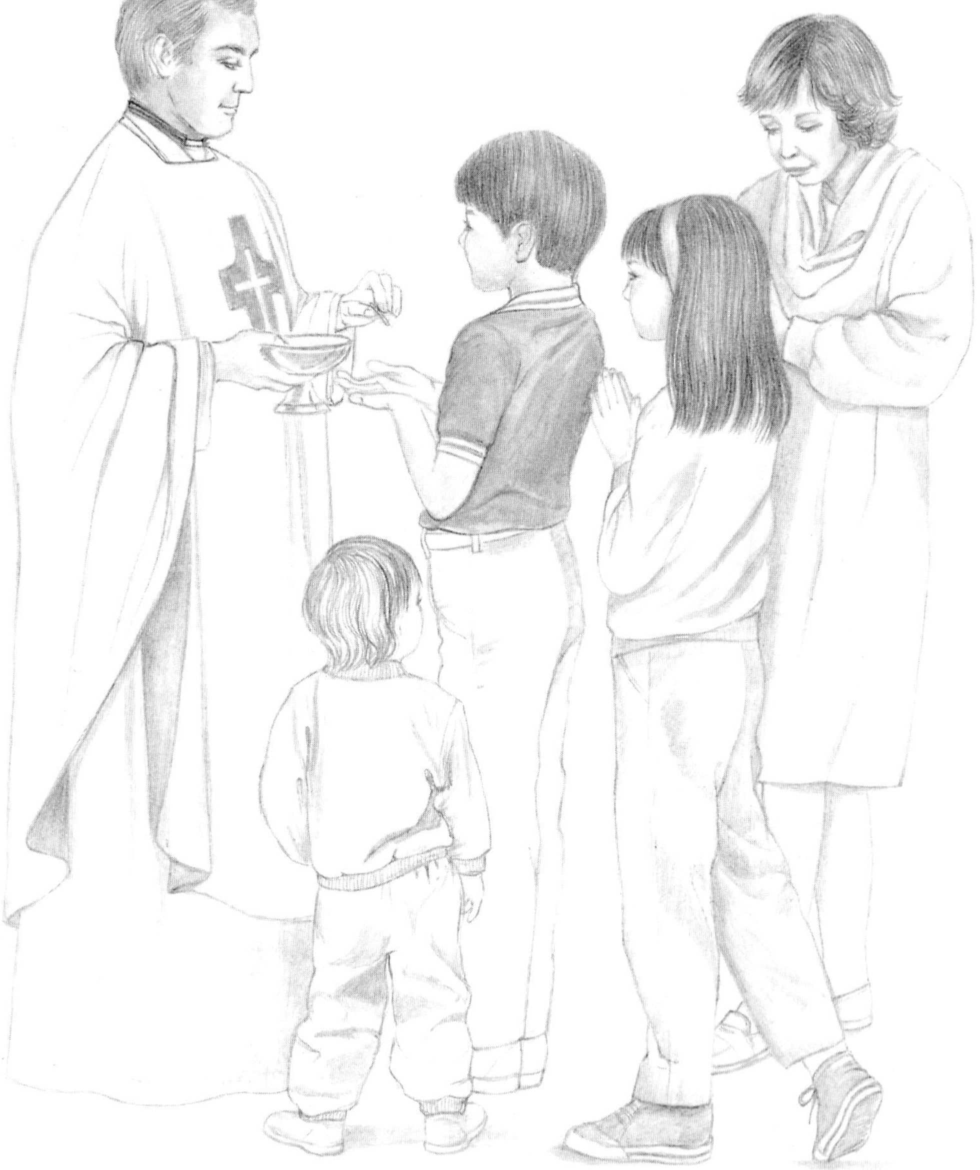

Sixteen

Communion Rite with Adults

OUR FATHER
With confidence we pray for the coming of the kingdom.

> Our Father, who art in heaven,
> hallowed be thy name.
> Thy kingdom come,
> thy will be done
> on earth as it is in heaven.
> Give us this day our daily bread,
> and forgive us our trespasses
> as we forgive those who trespass against us,
> and lead us not into temptation
> but deliver us from evil.

The priest concludes:

> Deliver us, Lord, from every evil,
> and grant us peace in our day.
> In your mercy keep us free from sin
> and protect us from all anxiety
> as we wait in joyful hope
> for the coming of our Saviour,
> Jesus Christ.

THE LORD BE WITH YOU

Everyone continues:

**For the Kingdom, the power and the
glory are yours, now and for ever.**

The priest continues, praying for peace and unity.

SIGN OF PEACE

We offer each other a sign of peace.

LAMB OF GOD *(This may be sung.)*

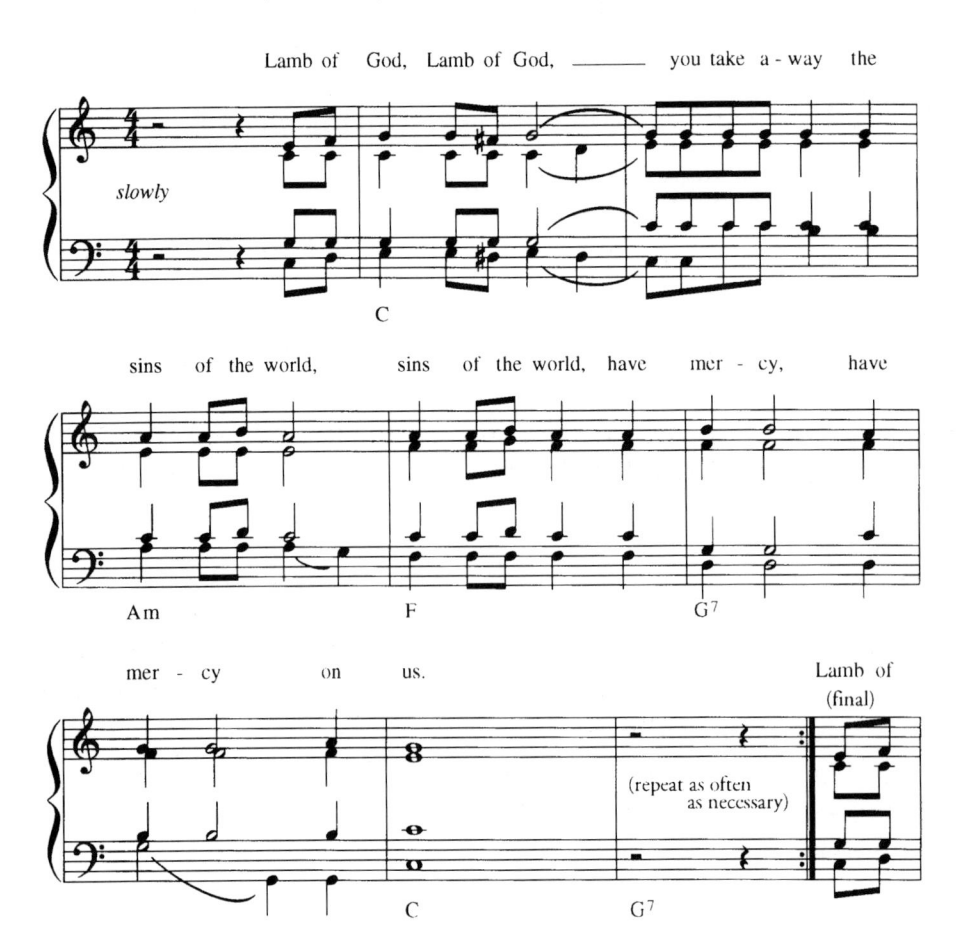

Lamb of God, Lamb of God, ——— you take a-way the sins of the world, sins of the world, have mer-cy, have mer-cy on us. Lamb of (final)

slowly

(repeat as often as necessary)

58

Sixteen – Communion Rite with Adults

God, Lamb of God, you take a-way the sins of the world, sins of the world. grant us, grant us peace.

Lamb of God: Garfield Rochard © McCrimmon Publishing Co.Ltd

(For alternative settings, please see Music resource section)

Whilst this is being said (or sung) the priest having broken a small part of the host, places it in the chalice; he then continues with the breaking of bread.

> When Jesus took the bread at the last supper, he blessed it, gave thanks, broke it and gave it to his disciples. This broken bread reminds us of the brokenness of Jesus' story. It reminds us of our brokenness. It reminds us that Jesus is present in the broken parts of life and because this is so, we need never give up hope. What was broken was made new. This will be true for us too. Jesus is risen and made new. Jesus has redeemed us.

INVITATION TO COMMUNION

The priest says,

> This is the Lamb of God who takes away the sins of the world. Happy are those who are called to his supper.

Or in similar words.

COMMUNION
Since the sign of the eucharistic meal appears more clearly, the sign of communion is more complete when given under both kinds.

PRAYER AFTER COMMUNION.
A final short prayer which again relates to the theme of the Mass.

Seventeen

Communion Rite with Children

This is a popular rite with children; it includes a familiar prayer and movement! Teachers and parents during a full celebration of the eucharist can now ease off exercising their "ministry of the glare", unless, having suffered from enforced stillness for a very long period, the children "go over the top" at the sign of peace.

The format remains the same:

OUR FATHER

> We pray that God's kingdom will come.

SING OF PEACE

> We begin to build it now.

LAMB OF GOD

> Jesus puts everything right, even the crummy parts of life and the greatest disappointments. We can put our trust in him.

COMMUNION

We join with Jesus and each other in this special way. God has made a promise, that one day we will be with him in heaven. We promise God, that we will serve him and do good, just like Jesus.

PRAYER AFTER COMMUNION

We pray for strength.

An exemplar:

> God our Father
> you give us a share in the one bread
> and the one cup and make us one with Jesus.
> Help us to bring your hope and joy
> to all the world.
> We ask this in the name of Jesus.
> **Amen**

Eighteen

Preparing the Communion Rite with Children

An optimum age for children to celebrate this rite is from about 7/8 years upwards, though of course this will vary from child to child.

A simple paraliturgy based on this rite, (such as the following) celebrated from time to time, may contribute to their understanding.

BEFORE YOU BEGIN

For ways of introducing and praying the Our Father, see *Kingdom Spotting* in "PRAYING WITH CHILDREN: Some Ways and Means" by Jenny Pate (published by McCrimmons ISBN 0 85597 5466)

With 7/8/9 year olds

On a large poster brainstorm all the ideas they associate with sin. Start by asking: "What is sin?"

On the other side of the poster, write all the ideas they associate with being good, asking: "What is goodness?" (If anger doesn't come up, suggest it, it is sometimes right and necessary to be angry.)

Make three posters.

THE LORD BE WITH YOU

With 10 and 11 year olds

List under the heading what

BREAD means:

_ _ _ _ _ _ _ _	_ _ _ _ _ _ _ _
_ _ _ _ _ _ _ _	_ _ _ _ _ _ _ _
_ _ _ _ _ _ _ _	_ _ _ _ _ _ _ _

e.g. money, food, a home, family, friends.

List some ways in which your "bread" is blessed.
List some ways in which your "bread" is broken and crummy.

Name a happy time; name a sad time.
Name a hope; name a disappointment.

NB: Children may choose to keep their thoughts confidential.

Explain the symbolism of the breaking of bread during the "Lamb of God".

Jesus is with us in bad time and good, in happy times and sad.

In the breaking of bread we remember that Jesus is present in the difficult times, and we remember his dying on the cross, his broken body.

- It might also be an appropriate time to explain why communion under both kinds is a more complete sign.

Through the shedding of blood (Jesus' death) the covenant, i.e. the promise of God was completed. This does not mean that God our Father wanted his son to have a horrible death, far from it!

Jesus is the complete sign of God. Everything he said and did was true to what God our Father would say and do. Sadly there were some people who didn't want to hear what Jesus had to say, they didn't agree with him, so they put him to death.

God our Father raised Jesus from the dead, proving that Jesus was right, he was speaking the truth!

Jesus did not choose to run away when he was captured (though he wanted to), because he wanted us to know the truth. He chose to stay and give himself to us completely. The Covenant was his LIFE as well as his death.

>His death said YES to the truth;
>YES to God's promise that we will know the truth.

>Jesus gave himself.
>Jesus is God.
>God gave himself to us.
>
>>Amazing!

Nineteen

Act of Worship based on the Communion Rite

Leader   Our act of worship is about building the kingdom of God, making the world a better place to live, the sort of place God intended it to be.

We begin with: Our Father…

Nineteen – Act of Worship based on the Communion Rite

SIGN OF PEACE

Child A Jesus you said to your disciples,
I leave you peace, my peace I give you.
Do not look at our sins:
instead look at the hope we have in you.
Please give us the peace and unity
of heaven, where you live.

Everyone **Amen.**

Child B Let's start now to build peace.
The peace of the Lord be with you always.

Everyone **And also with you.**

Child B Let us offer each other the sign of peace.

Once calm has resumed, three children with posters describing their ideas of sinfulness stand where they can be seen.

Child C Lamb of God, you take away the sins of the world:

> *[1st poster turned over to display ideas of goodness.]*

Everyone **Have mercy on us.**

Child D Lamb of God, you take away the sins of the world:

> *[2nd poster turned over.]*

Everyone **Have mercy on us.**

Child E Lamb of God, you take away the sins of the world.

> *[3rd poster turned over.]*

Everyone **Grant us peace.**

Child F Jesus is the Lamb of God, who takes away the sins of the world, happy are those called to work with him.

THE LORD BE WITH YOU

ACT OF COMMITMENT
Stand in a circle holding hands

> God our Father,
> Long ago you promised that you would show us the way to be happy.
> By sending Jesus you kept that promise.
>
> We promise to show others how to live
> the same way that Jesus did,
> so that one day we will all be happy with you
> in heaven.

FINAL PRAYER
(adapt using your own words)

> God,
> Your Son Jesus taught us to call you "Our Father".
> Please help us to live happily,
> to be like your Son.
> We ask this as friends of his. Amen.

You may like to conclude with a blessing (see the "Concluding Rite")

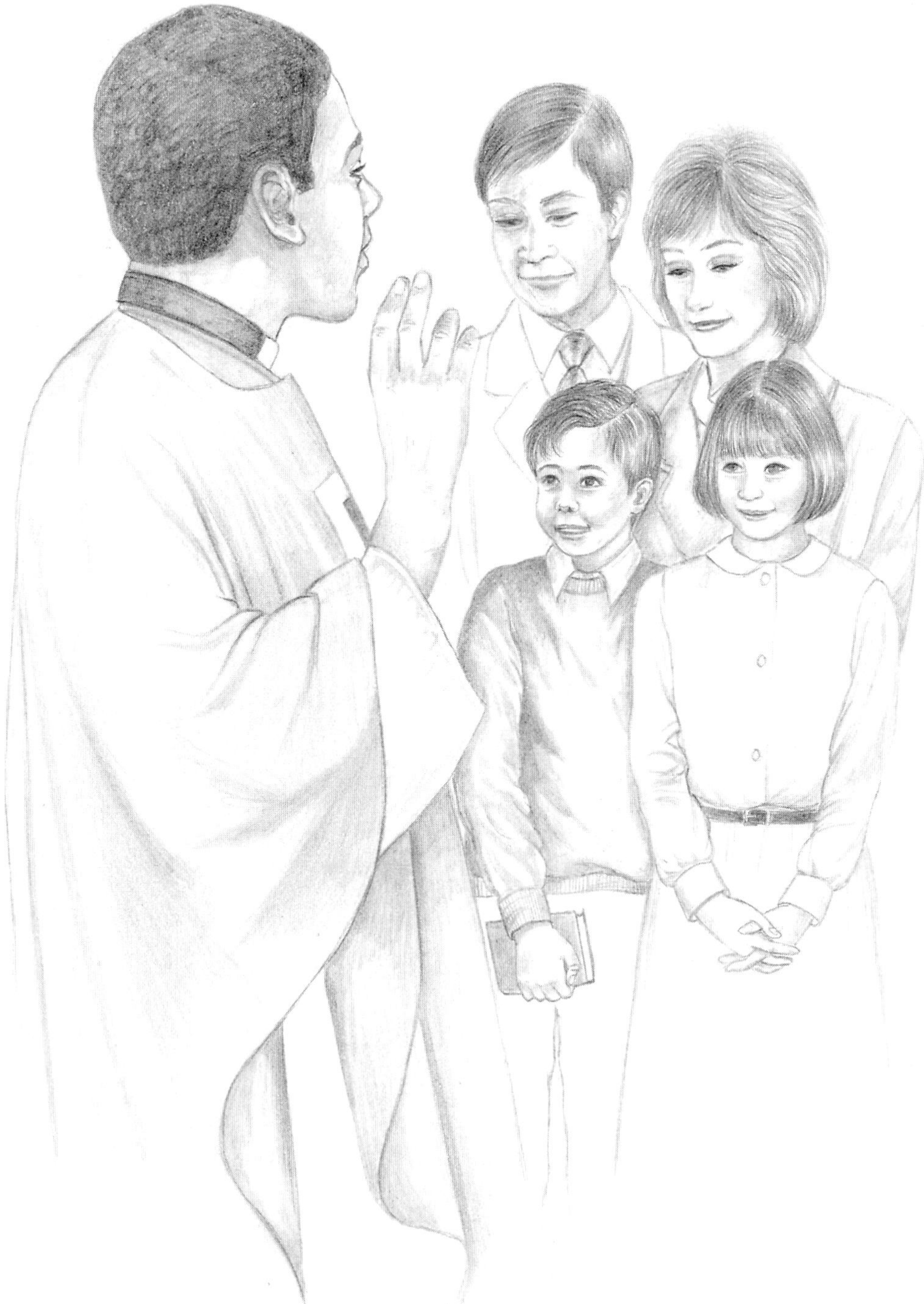

Twenty

Concluding Rite With Adults

The concluding rites simply consist of a blessing and, possibly, a recessional hymn. Any announcements are made at this point.

BLESSING

Priest The Lord be with you.

Everyone **And also with you.**

Priest May almighty God bless you, + the Father, and the Son, and the Holy Spirit. **Amen.**

Go in the peace of Christ.
or
The Mass is ended, go in peace.
or
Go in peace to love and serve the Lord.
Thanks be to God.

An alternative style:

An exemplar

Priest The Lord be with you.

Everyone **And also with you.**

Priest May the Father who provides be generous to us. **Amen.**

THE LORD BE WITH YOU

May the Son who teaches
guide us and show us the way. **Amen**

May the Spirit
encourage us when we lose heart. **Amen**

And may almighty God… *(as above)*

Twenty One

Concluding Rite With Children
Adapt, adapt, adapt!

A home time blessing at the end of the school day. Adapt, adapt, adapt!

Teacher The Lord be with you.

Children **And also with you.**

Teacher May God our Father
keep you safe
from all harm.
Amen.

May Jesus our brother
help you to know and
do what is right.
Amen.

May the Holy Spirit
give you courage when
you are tempted
to do wrong.
Amen.

THE LORD BE WITH YOU

Teacher And may almighty God bless you with all good things, the Father, the Son and the Holy Spirit.
Amen.

Teacher Go in peace to love and serve the Lord.

Everyone **Thanks be to God.**

At some point, bring to the children's attention the start of the blessing.
"The Lord be with you…"
It marks the beginning of something special, i.e. going home to love and serve the Lord.

Music resource section

This section provides suggestions for music to use during the children's liturgies. The selection of hymns and settings suggested below is taken from Celebration Hymnal for Everyone (CFE) and A Year of Celebration (YOC) and we have provided the corresponding numbers in these books, both published by McCrimmons.

In the case where neither of these publications is accessible to you, we have written out the music of two different Mass settings in this section for your convenience.

	CFE	YOC		CFE	YOC
Entrance/Gathering Songs			**Psalms**		
I will sing	291	104	Father, we adore you	164	114
This is the day	731	11	As the deer	54	135
We are gathering	767	12	All things bright		
Morning has broken	490	7	and beautiful	27	15
Here in this place	253	–	The Lord is my shepherd	705	–
			The Lord's my shepherd	706	–
Penitential Rite			Jubilate	338	–
Lord, have mercy	402	–	Blest be the Lord	91	–
Look around you	376	51	**Gospel Acclamation**		
Lord, have mercy					
(Mass of Peace)	404	–	Jesus is risen	–	183
			Celtic Alleluia	410	–
Gloria			Glory and praise		
Gloria (Anderson)	408	181	(for use in Lent)	414	–
Gloria (Milton)	–	182			
Gloria (Mass of Peace)	405	–			

THE LORD BE WITH YOU

	CFE	YOC		CFE	YOC
Offertory songs			**Eucharistic Acclamation**		
We bring our gifts	–	186	Glory to God (Milton)	–	182
All that I am	23	–	**Great Amen**		
In bread we bring you, Lord	302	–	Amen *(music given below)*	451	–
Take our bread	678	–	**Lamb of God**		
Here I am, Lord	285	–	Jesus, you are Bread	–	192
Holy, holy			Communion Song 3	452	–
Celtic Holy, holy	422	–	Lamb of God (Mass of Peace)	456	–
Holy, holy (Mass of Peace)	442	–			

Music resource section

Mass settings

Israeli Mass

Christ, have mercy...

Lord, have mercy...

Holy, holy, holy

Holy, holy, holy, holy,
Lord of power, Lord of might.
Heav'n and earth are filled with glory.
Sing hosanna evermore.

Blest and holy, blest and holy,
he who comes from God on high.
Raise your voices, sing his glory,
praise his name for evermore.

Lamb of God

Lamb of God,
 you take away
 the sin, the sin of all the world.
Give us mercy,
 give us mercy,
 give us mercy, Lamb of God. *(Repeat)*

Lamb of God,
 you take away
 the sin, the sin of all the world.
Grant us peace, Lord,
 grant us peace, Lord,
 grant us peace, O Lamb of God.

Anthony Hamson

American Eucharist

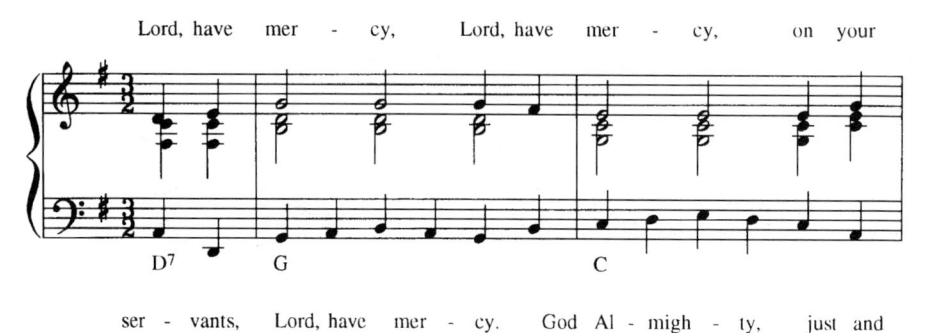

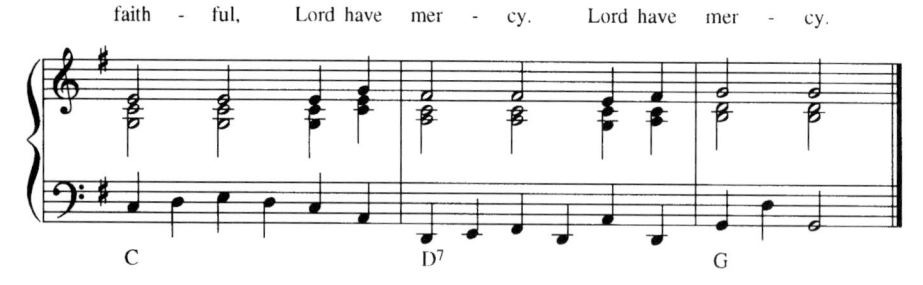

Lord, have mercy, Lord, have mercy, on your servants, Lord, have mercy. God Almighty, just and faithful, Lord have mercy. Lord have mercy.

Christ, have mercy...

Lord, have mercy...

Holy, holy, holy

Holy, holy, holy, holy,
Lord of hosts. You fill with glory
all the earth and all the heavens.
Sing hosanna, sing hosanna.

Blest and holy, blest and holy
he who comes now in the Lord's name.
In the highest sing hosanna,
In the highest sing hosanna.

Lamb of God

Jesus, Lamb of God, have mercy,
bearer of our sins, have mercy. *(twice)*

Saviour of the world, Lord Jesus,
may your peace be with us always. *(twice)*

Sandra Joan Billington

Amen